THE POWER OF SOLITUDE

A GUIDE TO EMBRACING LONELINESS

PREVIEW

Welcome to a journey of self-discovery and introspection. In a world that often values noise and distraction, this book invites you to explore the power of solitude. Within these pages, we'll delve into the benefits of embracing quiet time, from increased creativity and productivity to improved mental health and well-being. Solitude is not about isolation or loneliness; it's about cultivating a deeper understanding of yourself and the world around you. Through solitude, you can tap into your inner strength, foster meaningful connections, and live a more authentic life.

In the following chapters, we'll explore the many facets of solitude, from its role in personal growth and creativity to its impact on mental health and relationships. Whether you're looking to reduce stress, boost your creativity, or simply find more balance in your life, this book offers practical insights and guidance to help you harness the power of solitude.

As you embark on this journey, remember that solitude is a personal and subjective experience. It's not about following a specific formula or achieving a particular outcome; it's about embracing the quiet moments and allowing yourself to grow, learn, and evolve. I hope that this book will inspire you to prioritize solitude in your life and discover the many benefits it has to offer.

TABLE OF CONTENTS

Chapter 1: The Benefits of Solitude
Introduction

In today's fast-paced world, solitude is often viewed as a negative state, something to be avoided at all costs. We're constantly connected to our devices, social media, and the people around us. But what if I told you that solitude can be a powerful tool for personal growth, creativity, and well-being? In this chapter, we'll explore the benefits of solitude and why it's essential for a happy and fulfilling life.

Solitude is not about being lonely; it's about being alone with your thoughts, emotions, and desires. It's about taking time to reflect, recharge, and renew yourself. In today's fast-paced world, solitude is often viewed as a luxury, but it's actually a necessity. By embracing solitude, we can gain a deeper understanding of ourselves, tap into our creativity, and improve our mental health.

Think about it. When was the last time you took a walk alone, without your phone or any distractions? When was the last time you sat in silence, without any noise or interruptions? If you're like most people, it's probably been a while. But solitude is essential for our well-being, and it's time we start prioritizing it in our lives.

In this chapter, we'll explore the benefits of solitude and why it's essential for a happy and fulfilling life. We'll look at the science behind solitude, real-life examples of people who have benefited from it, and practical ways to cultivate it in our daily lives. You'll understand why solitude is not just a luxury, but a necessity for anyone looking to live a more meaningful and creative.

The Benefits of Solitude

1. Increased Self-Awareness :

Solitude allows us to tune into our thoughts, emotions, and desires. By spending time alone, we can gain a deeper understanding of ourselves, our values, and our goals.

2. Improved Creativity :

Solitude provides the space for our minds to explore new ideas, and think outside the box. Many famous artists, writers, and innovators have credited solitude with sparking their creativity.

3. Better Mental Health :

Solitude can be a powerful tool for managing stress, anxiety, and depression. By taking time for ourselves, we can recharge, reflect, and gain a new perspective on life.

4. Increased Productivity :

Solitude can help us focus, prioritize, and accomplish our goals. Without distractions, we can work more efficiently and effectively.

5. Deeper Connections :

Paradoxically, solitude can actually help us form deeper connections with others. By taking time to reflect on our relationships and values, we can build stronger, more meaningful bonds with those around us.

The Science Behind Solitude :

Research has shown that solitude can have a positive impact on our brains and bodies. For example, studies have found that solitude can:

- Reduce stress hormones .
- Increase activity in areas of the brain associated with creativity and problem-solving
- Improves sleep quality .
- Boosts immune function .

Real-Life Examples

Many successful people have credited solitude with helping them achieve their goals. For example: .

- Steve Jobs, co-founder of Apple, was known for his love of solitude and meditation.
- Albert Einstein, the famous physicist, often spent hours alone in his study, thinking and reflecting.
- Maya Angelou, the renowned author, would often spend time alone in a hotel room to focus on her writing.. .

Conclusion

In this chapter, we've explored the benefits of solitude and why it's essential for a happy and fulfilling life. By embracing solitude, we can increase our self-awareness, improve our creativity, and boost our mental health.

Chapter 2: The Difference Between solitude and Loneliness

Introduction

In the previous chapter, we explored the benefits of solitude and why it's essential for a happy and fulfilling life. However, many people struggle to distinguish between solitude and loneliness. While solitude is a state of being alone by choice, loneliness is a state of feeling isolated and disconnected from others. In this chapter, we'll delve into the differences between solitude and loneliness, and why understanding these differences is crucial for our mental and emotional well-being.

The Difference Between Solitude and Loneliness

1. Solitude is a choice .Solitude is a state of being alone that we choose for ourselves. It's a deliberate decision to spend time alone, whether it's to relax, reflect, or pursue a hobby.   .

2. Loneliness is a feeling : Loneliness, on the other hand, is a feeling of isolation and disconnection from others. It's a negative emotional state that can be triggered by a variety of factors, including social isolation, loss, or trauma.   .

3. Solitude is rejuvenating : Solitude can be rejuvenating and restorative, allowing us to recharge and refocus. Loneliness, by contrast, can be draining and debilitating, leaving us feeling empty   and   disconnected.

4. Solitude is empowering : Solitude can be empowering, allowing us to take control of our lives and make choices that nourish our   minds, .

bodies, and spirits. Loneliness, on the other hand, can be disempowering, leaving us feeling helpless and disconnected from others.

The Psychology of Loneliness :

Loneliness is a complex and multifaceted emotion that can have serious consequences for our mental and physical health. Research has shown that chronic loneliness can:

☐ Increase the risk of depression, anxiety, and other mental health disorders
☐ weakening the immune system
☐ Increase blood pressure and cardio disease .
☐ Reduce cognitive function and increase the risk of dementia

The Benefits of Embracing Solitude :

By contrast, embracing solitude can have numerous benefits for our mental and emotional well-being. Solitude can:

- Increase self-awareness and introspection
- Foster creativity and problem-solving
- Improve mental clarity and focus
- Enhance self-esteem and confidence

Real-Life Examples :

Many people have benefited from embracing solitude, including:

- Authors like JK Rowling and Stephen King, who have credited solitude with helping them write bestselling novels.
- Artists like Vincent van Gogh and Frida Kahlo, who used solitude to fuel their creativity
- Entrepreneurs and business leaders, who often use solitude to reflect and strategize

Conclusion

In this chapter, we've explored the differences between solitude and loneliness, and why understanding these differences is crucial for our mental and emotional well-being. By embracing solitude and recognizing the signs of loneliness, we can take steps to nurture our minds, bodies, and spirits. In the following chapters, we'll explore practical ways to cultivate solitude and build meaningful connections with others.

Chapter 3: The History and Philosophy of Solitude

Introduction

Solitude has been a part of human experience for thousands of years, with many cultures and philosophers exploring its benefits and significance. From ancient Greek philosophers to modern-day spiritual leaders, solitude has been recognized as a powerful tool for personal growth, creativity, and spiritual development. In this chapter, we'll explore the history and philosophy of solitude, and how it has been understood and practiced across different cultures and traditions.

The Ancient Roots of Solitude

1. Ancient Greece and Rome : Philosophers like Epicurus, Aristotle, and Seneca wrote about the importance of solitude for personal growth, creativity, and wisdom.

2. Eastern Spiritual Traditions : In Buddhism, Taoism, and Hinduism, solitude is often seen as a means of spiritual development, allowing individuals to cultivate mindfulness, wisdom, and inner peace.

3. Christian Hermits : In the early Christian tradition, hermits and monks would often retreat to the desert or wilderness to pray, reflect, and seek spiritual guidance.

The Philosophical Significance of Solitude

1. Existentialism : Existentialist philosophers like Jean-Paul Sartre and Martin Heidegger emphasized the importance of individual

freedom and responsibility, often finding solitude to be a necessary condition for authentic existence.

2. Romanticism : Romantic writers and artists often celebrated the beauty and power of nature, finding solitude to be a source of inspiration and creativity.

3. Stoicism : Stoic philosophers like Epictetus and Marcus Aurelius emphasized the importance of inner strength, resilience, and self-awareness, often cultivating solitude as a means of developing these qualities.

The Benefits of Solitude in History

1. Creative Breakthroughs : Many famous artists, writers, and musicians have credited solitude with helping them make creative breakthroughs and produce their best work.

2. Spiritual Growth : Solitude has been used by spiritual seekers across cultures and traditions to deepen their understanding of themselves and the world around them.

3. Personal Growth : Solitude has been recognized as a powerful tool for personal growth, allowing individuals to develop greater self-awareness, self-discipline, and emotional intelligence.

Modern Perspectives on Solitude :

1. The Digital Age : In today's digital age, solitude is often seen as a luxury or a rarity, with many people feeling pressure to be constantly connected and available.

2. Mental Health : Solitude is increasingly recognized as an important aspect of mental health, allowing individuals to recharge, reflect, and prioritize their well-being.

3. Sustainability : Solitude can also be seen as a sustainable practice, allowing individuals to live more simply, mindfully, and in harmony with nature.

Conclusion

In this chapter, we've explored the history and philosophy of solitude, and how it has been understood and practiced across different cultures and traditions. By recognizing the significance of solitude in human experience, we can begin to appreciate its value and importance in our own lives. In the following chapters, we'll explore practical ways to cultivate solitude and make it a part of our daily lives.

Chapter 4. Setting Bounds and Prioritizing Alone Time

Introduction

In today's fast-paced world, it's easy to get caught up in the demands of others and neglect our own needs. Setting boundaries and prioritizing alone time is essential for maintaining our physical, emotional, and mental well-being. In this chapter, we'll explore the importance of setting boundaries and prioritizing alone time, and provide practical tips for doing so.

The Importance of Setting Boundaries

1. Protecting Your Time and Energy : Setting boundaries helps you protect your time and energy from being drained by others. By prioritizing your own needs, you can maintain your physical and mental health.

2. Building Healthy Relationships : Setting boundaries is essential for building healthy relationships. By communicating your needs and limits clearly, you can avoid conflicts and build stronger, more respectful relationships.

3. Increasing Self-Esteem : Setting boundaries can help you develop greater self-esteem and confidence.

Prioritizing Alone Time

1. Scheduling Alone Time : Prioritizing alone time means scheduling time for yourself, whether it's reading, meditating, or simply taking a walk. By making alone time a priority, you can recharge and refocus.

2. Learning to Say No : Prioritizing alone time also means learning to say no to others when necessary. By setting boundaries and prioritizing your own needs, you can avoid over committing and maintain your energy.

3. Creating a Safe Space : Prioritizing alone time means creating a safe space for yourself, whether it's a quiet room in your home or a peaceful outdoor spot. By creating a safe space, you can relax and recharge.

Practical Tips for Setting Boundaries and Prioritizing Alone Time

1. Communicate Your Needs : Communicate your needs and limits clearly to others, whether it's a family member, friend, or colleague.

2. Set Realistic Expectations : Set realistic expectations with others about what you can and can't do. By being clear about your limits, you can avoid over committing and maintain your energy.

3. Prioritize Self-Care : Prioritize self-care activities like exercise, meditation, and spending time in nature. By taking care of your physical and emotional needs, you can maintain your overall well-being.   .

4. Learn to Say No : Learn to say no to others when necessary. By setting boundaries and prioritizing your own needs, you can avoid over committing and maintain your energy.   .

Overcoming Obstacles

1. Guilt and Shame : Many people feel guilty or ashamed about prioritizing alone time. However, it's essential to remember that taking care of yourself is not selfish, but necessary.   .

2. Fear of Rejection : Some people may fear that setting boundaries will lead to rejection or conflict. However, setting boundaries is essential for building healthy relationships and maintaining your own well-being.   .

3. Lack of Time : Many people feel like they don't have enough time to prioritize alone time. However, even small amounts of alone time can be beneficial, such as taking a few minutes each day to meditate or read.   .

Conclusion

In this chapter, we've explored the importance of setting boundaries and prioritizing alone time. By setting boundaries and prioritizing your own needs, you can maintain your physical, emotional, and mental well-being. By following the practical tips outlined in this chapter, you can start prioritizing alone time and setting boundaries in your own life.   .

Chapter 5: Creating a Solitude-Friendly Environment

Introduction

Creating a solitude-friendly environment is essential for cultivating solitude and making it a part of your daily life. A solitude-friendly environment is a space that promotes relaxation, reflection, and rejuvenation, allowing you to disconnect from the world and reconnect with yourself. In this chapter, we'll explore the importance of creating a solitude-friendly environment   .

The Importance of a Solitude-Friendly Environment

1. Promoting Relaxation : A solitude-friendly environment can promote relaxation and reduce stress, allowing you to unwind and recharge.   .

2. Fostering Reflection : A solitude-friendly environment can foster reflection and introspection, allowing you to gain insights into your thoughts, feelings, and behaviors.   .

3. Encouraging Creativity : A solitude-friendly environment can encourage creativity and imagination, allowing you to express yourself and explore new ideas.   .

Designing a Solitude-Friendly Space

1. Minimalism : A solitude-friendly space often features minimalism, with a focus on simplicity and clarity. By removing clutter and distractions, you can create a space that promotes relaxation and focus.   .

2. Nature : Incorporating nature into your solitude-friendly space can be beneficial,
.

whether it's a view of the outdoors or a plant-filled room. Nature can promote feelings of calm and well-being.   .

3. Comfort : A solitude-friendly space should be comfortable and inviting, with a focus on creating a sense of safety and security. This can include features like soft lighting, comfortable seating, and soothing colors.

Practical Tips for Creating a Solitude -Friendly Environment

1. De-clutter Your Space : De-clutter your space by removing unnecessary items and distractions. This can help promote relaxation and focus.

2. Create a Quiet Space : Create a quiet space by using noise-canceling materials or finding a quiet location. This can help you focus and relax.

3. Incorporate Nature : Incorporate nature into your solitude-friendly space by adding plants, viewing the outdoors, or using natural materials.

4. Make it Comfortable : Make your solitude-friendly space comfortable by adding soft lighting, comfortable seating, and soothing colors.

Overcoming Obstacles

1. Limited Space : If you have limited space, consider creating a solitude-friendly corner or nook. This can be a designated area for relaxation and reflection.

2. Distractions : If you're easily distracted, consider using tools like noise-canceling headphones or a meditation app to help you focus.

3. Technology : Consider setting boundaries around technology use in your solitude-friendly space. This can help you disconnect and focus on your inner experience.

Conclusion

In this chapter, we've explored the importance of creating a solitude-friendly environment and provided practical tips for doing so. By designing a space that promotes relaxation, reflection, and creativity, you can cultivate solitude and make it a part of your daily life. Whether you're looking to reduce stress, increase productivity, or simply find more joy in life, a solitude-friendly environment can be a powerful tool for achieving your goals.

Chapter 6: Engaging in Solo Activities

Introduction

Engaging in solo activities is an essential part of cultivating solitude and making it a part of your daily life. Solo activities can help you relax, reflect, and recharge, allowing you to connect with yourself and the world around you. In this chapter, we'll explore the benefits of engaging in solo activities and provide practical tips for incorporating them into your life.

Benefits of Solo Activities

1. Relaxation : Solo activities can help you relax and reduce stress, allowing you to unwind and recharge.

2. Reflection : Solo activities can foster reflection and introspection, allowing you to gain insights into your thoughts, feelings, and behaviors.

3. Creativity : Solo activities can encourage creativity and imagination, allowing you to express yourself and explore new ideas.

Solo Activities

1. Reading : Reading can be a great solo activity, allowing you to escape into a different world and gain new insights.

2. Writing : Writing can be a powerful solo activity, allowing you to express yourself and reflect on your experiences.

3. Meditation and Mindfulness : Meditation and mindfulness can be excellent solo activities, allowing you to cultivate inner peace and calm.

4. Creative Pursuits : Engaging in creative pursuits like painting, drawing, or playing music can be a great way to express yourself and tap into your creativity.   .

Practical Tips for Engaging in Solo Activities

1. Schedule Solo Time : Schedule solo time into your daily or weekly routine, making sure to prioritize your own needs.   .

2. Experiment with Different Activities : Experiment with different solo activities to find what works best for you.   .

3. Create a Conductive Environment : Create a conductive environment for solo activities, whether it's a quiet space or a comfortable spot in nature.   .

4. Be Consistent : Be consistent in your solo activities, making them a regular part of your routine.   .

Overcoming Obstacles

1. Feeling Guilty : Many people feel guilty about taking time for themselves. However, solo activities can be beneficial for your mental and emotional   well-being.   .
2. Lack of Motivation : If you're struggling to find motivation for solo activities, try starting small or finding activities that bring you joy.   .
3. Distractions : If you're easily distracted, try to minimize distractions by finding a quiet space or using tools like noise-canceling headphones.   .

Conclusion

In this chapter, we've explored the benefits of engaging in solo activities and provided practical tips for incorporating them into your life. By prioritizing solo activities, you can cultivate solitude and make it a part of your daily life. Whether you're looking to relax, reflect, or express yourself creatively, solo activities can be a powerful tool for achieving your   goals.   .

Chapter 7: Overcoming the Stigma of Solitude
Introduction

Despite the many benefits of solitude, there is often a stigma associated with it. Many people view solitude as a negative state, associated with loneliness, isolation, or social awkwardness. However, solitude can be a powerful tool for personal growth, creativity, and well-being. In this chapter, we'll explore the stigma of loneliness and provide practical tips for overcoming it.

The Stigma of Solitude

1. Societal Pressure : Societal pressure to be social and connected can make it difficult for people to prioritize solitude. Many people feel like they need to be constantly connected to others, whether it's through social media or in-person interactions.

2. Fear of Judgment : The fear of being judged or misunderstood can also contribute to the stigma of solitude. Some people may view solitude as a sign of weakness or lack of social skills.

3. Cultural Norms : Cultural norms around social interaction can also play a role in the stigma of solitude. In some cultures, solitude is viewed as a luxury or a privilege, rather than a necessary part of life.

Overcoming the Stigma of Solitude

1. Reframing Solitude : One way to overcome the stigma of solitude is to reframe it in a positive light. Instead of viewing solitude as a negative state, try to see it as an opportunity for growth, reflection, and creativity.

2. Prioritizing Self-Care : Prioritizing self-care and recognizing the importance of solitude for mental and emotional well-being can also help to overcome the stigma.

3. Finding Supportive Communities : Finding supportive communities or like-minded individuals who value solitude can also help to reduce the stigma.

Practical Tips for Overcoming the Stigma of Solitude

1. Start Small : Start small by incorporating short periods of solitude into your daily routine.

2. Communicate with Others : Communicate with others about your needs and boundaries, and prioritize your own well-being.

3. Focus on the Benefits : Focus on the benefits of solitude, such as increased productivity, creativity, and self-awareness.

4.   Practice   Self-Compassion   :   Practice self-compassion and recognize that it's okay to prioritize your own needs.   .

Conclusion

In this chapter, we've explored the stigma of solitude   and   provided   practical   tips   for overcoming it. By reframing solitude in a positive light, prioritizing self-care, and finding supportive communities, you can overcome the stigma and cultivate a more positive relationship with   solitude.   .

Chapter 8: Building Self-Compassion and Self-Acceptance

Introduction

Building self-compassion and self-acceptance is essential for cultivating a positive relationship with solitude. When we practice self-compassion and self-acceptance, we're better able to navigate the challenges of solitude and reap its benefits. In this chapter, we'll explore the importance of self-compassion and self-acceptance, and provide practical tips for building these qualities.

The Importance of Self-Compassion and Self -Acceptance

1. Reducing Self-Criticism : Self-compassion and self-acceptance can help reduce self-criticism and increase self-kindness.

2. Increasing Resilience : Practicing self-compassion and self-acceptance can also increase resilience and ability to cope with challenges.

3. Improving Relationships : By cultivating self-compassion and self-acceptance, we can also improve our relationships with others.

Practical Tips for Building Self-Compassion and Self -Acceptance

1. Practice Mindfulness : Mindfulness can help us become more aware of our thoughts and feelings, and cultivate self-compassion and self-acceptance.

2. Use Kind Language : Using kind language when speaking to ourselves can help cultivate self-compassion and self-acceptance.

3. Focus on Strengths : Focusing on our strengths and accomplishments can help build self-acceptance and self-esteem.   .
4. Practice Self-Care : Practicing self-care and prioritizing our own needs can also help build self-compassion and self-acceptance.   .

Overcoming Obstacles

1. Self-Criticism : One of the biggest obstacles to building self -compassion and self -acceptance is self -criticism. By practicing mindfulness and using kind language, we can overcome self-criticism and cultivate a more positive relationship with ourselves.   .

2. Negative Self-Talk : Negative self-talk can also be a major obstacle. By focusing on strengths and accomplishments, and practicing self-care, we can overcome negative self-talk and build self-compassion and self-acceptance.

Conclusion

In this chapter, we've explored the importance of self-compassion and self-acceptance, and provided practical tips for building these qualities. By practicing mindfulness, using kind language, focusing on strengths, and practicing self-care, we can cultivate self-compassion and self-acceptance, and improve our relationships with ourselves and others.   .

Chapter 9: Finding Community and Support

Introduction

While solitude can be beneficial for personal growth and reflection, it's also important to have a supportive community and network of people who can provide connection and understanding. In this chapter, we'll explore the importance of finding community and support, and provide practical tips for building and maintaining these relationships.

The Importance of Community and Support

1. Emotional Support : Having a supportive community can provide emotional support and help us navigate challenging times.

2. Different Perspectives : Being part of a community can also provide different perspectives and insights, helping us grow and learn.

3. Sense of Belonging : Community and support can give us a sense of belonging, which is essential for our emotional and mental well-being.

Types of Community and Support

1. In-Person Communities : In-person communities, such as friends, family, and support groups, can provide face-to-face interaction and connection.

2. Online Communities : Online communities, such as social media groups and forums, can provide connection and support for people who may not have access to in-person communities.

3. Mentorship : Having a mentor or role model can provide guidance and support, helping us navigate challenges and achieve our goals.

Practical Tips for Finding Community and Support

1. Join a Group or Club : Joining a group or club that aligns with your interests can be a great way to meet new people and build connections.
2. Attend Events and Meetups : Attending events and meetups can provide opportunities to meet new people and build relationships.
3. Reach Out to Others : Reaching out to others, whether it's a friend, family member, or acquaintance, can help build connections and strengthen relationships.
4. Be Open and Authentic : Being open and authentic can help build trust and deepen relationships.

Overcoming Obstacles

1. Shyness or Social Anxiety : For people who are shy or experience social anxiety, building community and support can be challenging. Starting small, such as online communities or small groups, can help build confidence.
2. Time Constraints : Finding time to build community and support can be challenging. Prioritizing relationships and scheduling time for connection can help.
3. Fear of Rejection : Fear of rejection can hold people back from building community and support. Being open and authentic, and focusing on shared interests and values, can help build connections.

Conclusion

In this chapter, we've explored the importance of finding community and support, and provided practical tips for building and maintaining these relationships. By joining groups, attending events, reaching out to others, and being open and authentic, we can build a supportive community and network of people who can provide connection and understanding.

Chapter 10: Solitude and Creativity

Introduction

Solitude and creativity have long been linked, with many artists, writers, and musicians finding that solitude provides the perfect environment for inspiration and innovation. In this chapter, we'll explore the relationship between solitude and creativity, and provide practical tips for using solitude to boost your creative output.

The Relationship Between Solitude and Creativity

1. Freedom to Explore : Solitude provides the freedom to explore new ideas and take risks without fear of judgment or criticism. .
2. Increased Focus : Solitude can help increase focus and concentration, allowing you to dive deeper into your creative work. .
3. Access to the subconscious .Solitude can provide access to the subconscious mind, where creative ideas and insights often reside.

How Solitude Can Boost Creativity

1. Daydreaming : Solitude provides the perfect environment for daydreaming, .
.which can lead to new ideas and insights.
2. Experimentation : Solitude allows for experimentation and trying new things without fear of failure. .
3. Reflection : Solitude provides the opportunity for reflection, which can help you identify patterns and connections that might not be immediately apparent. .

Practical Tips for Using Solitude to Boost Creativity

1. Schedule Solitude : Schedule solitude into your daily or weekly routine, making sure to prioritize time for creative work. .

2. Create a Conducive Environment : Create a conductive environment for creativity, whether it's a quiet space or a clutter-free workspace. .

3. Practice Mindfulness : Practice mindfulness and meditation to tap into your subconscious mind and access creative ideas. .

4. Take Risks : Take risks and try new things, even if they might not work out. .

Examples of Creative Who Have Used Solitude

1. Authors : Many authors, such as JK Rowling and Stephen King, have credited solitude with helping them write their best work.

2. Artists : Artists like Vincent van Gogh and Frida Kahlo have used solitude to explore new ideas and techniques.   .

3. Musicians : Musicians like Brian Eno and Joni Mitchell have used solitude to compose and record music.   .

Conclusion

In this chapter, we've explored the relationship between solitude and creativity, and provided practical tips for using solitude to boost your creative output. By scheduling solitude, creating a conducive environment, practicing mindfulness, and taking risks, you can tap into your creative potential and produce your best work.   .

Chapter 11: Solitude and Personal Growth
Introduction

Solitude can be a powerful catalyst for personal growth, allowing us to reflect on our values, goals, and aspirations. In this chapter, we'll explore the relationship between solitude and personal growth, and provide practical tips for using solitude to promote self -awareness, self -acceptance, and self -improvement.

The Relationship Between Solitude and Personal Growth

1. Increased Self-Awareness : Solitude can increase self-awareness, allowing us to better understand our thoughts, feelings, and behaviors.

2. Reflection and Introspection : Solitude provides the opportunity for reflection and introspection, helping us to identify areas for personal growth and development.

3. Self-Acceptance : Solitude can promote self-acceptance, allowing us to develop a more positive and compassionate relationship with ourselves.

How Solitude Can Promote Personal Growth

1. Identifying Values and Goals : Solitude can help us identify our values and goals, and align them with our actions and decisions.

2. Developing Emotional Intelligence : Solitude can help us develop emotional intelligence, allowing us to better understand and manage our emotions.

3. Building Resilience : Solitude can help us build resilience, allowing us to better cope with challenges and setbacks.

Practical Tips for Using Solitude for Personal Growth

1. Schedule Regular Solitude Time : Schedule regular solitude time, whether it's daily, weekly, or monthly, to reflect on your thoughts, feelings, and behaviors.
2. Practice Journaling : Practice journaling or writing to reflect on your experiences and gain insights into your thoughts and feelings.
3. Engage in Self-Care : Engage in self-care activities, such as meditation or yoga, to promote relaxation and reduce stress.
4. Set Personal Goals : Set personal goals and work toward achieving them, using solitude as a time for reflection and planning.

Examples of Personal Growth Through Solitude

1. Increased Confidence : Solitude can help increase confidence, allowing us to take risks and pursue our goals and aspirations.
2. Improved Relationships : others .Solitude can help improve relationships, by allowing us to better understand ourselves and others.

3. Greater Sense of Purpose : Solitude can help us develop a greater sense of purpose, allowing us to live a more meaningful and fulfilling life.   .

Conclusion

In this chapter, we've explored the relationship between solitude and personal growth, and provided practical tips for using solitude to promote self-awareness, self-acceptance, and self-improvement. By scheduling regular solitude time, practicing journaling, engaging in self-care, and setting personal goals, you can use solitude as a catalyst for personal growth and   development.   .

Chapter 12: Solitude and Mental Health

Introduction

Solitude can have a profound impact on our mental health, both positively and negatively. In this chapter, we'll explore the complex relationship between solitude and mental health, and provide practical tips for using solitude to promote mental well-being.

The Relationship Between Solitude and Mental Health

1. Reducing Stress and Anxiety : Solitude can provide a much-needed break from the stresses of daily life, reducing feelings of anxiety and overwhelm.

2. Increasing Self-Awareness : Solitude can increase self-awareness, allowing us to better understand our thoughts, feelings, and behaviors.

3. Potential Risks : However, excessive solitude can also have negative effects on mental health, such as increased feelings of loneliness, isolation, and disconnection.

The Benefits of Solitude for Mental Health

1. Improved Mood : Solitude can improve our mood, allowing us to recharge and refocus.

2. Increased Productivity : Solitude can increase productivity, allowing us to focus on tasks and projects without distraction.

3. Better Sleep : Solitude can also promote better sleep, which is essential for mental health.

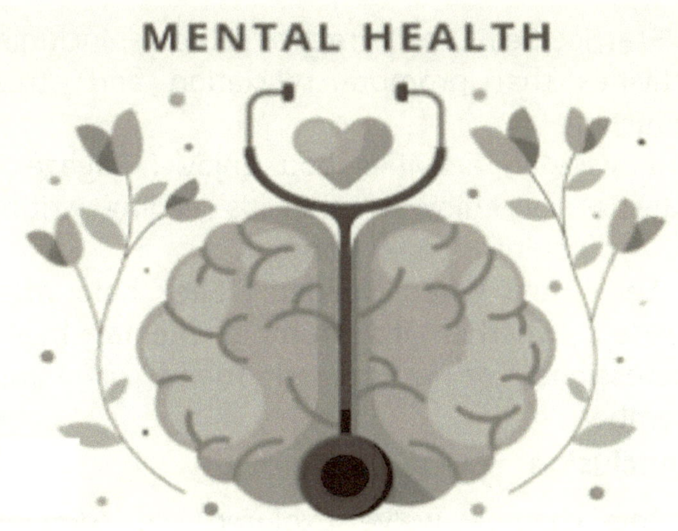

The Risks of Excessive Solitude

1. Loneliness and Isolation : Excessive solitude can lead to feelings of loneliness and isolation, which can negatively impact mental health.   .

2. Depression and Anxiety : Excessive solitude can also contribute to depression and anxiety, particularly if it is accompanied by negative thought   patterns.   .

3. Social Withdrawal : Excessive solitude can lead to social withdrawal, which can further exacerbate   mental   health   issues.   .

Practical Tips for Using Solitude to Promote Mental Health

1. Balance Solitude with Social Connection : Balance solitude with social connection, making sure to stay connected with friends, family,   and   community.   .

2. Practice Self-Care : Practice self-care, including activities that promote relaxation and stress reduction.

3. Engage in activities You Enjoy : Engage in activities you enjoy, whether it's reading, writing, or pursuing a hobby.   .

4. Seek Help When Needed : Seek help when needed, whether it's from a mental health professional or a trusted friend or family member.

Conclusion

In this chapter, we've explored the complex relationship between solitude and mental health, and provided practical tips for using solitude to promote mental well-being. By balancing solitude with social connection, practicing self-care, engaging in activities you enjoy, and seeking help when needed, you can use solitude to promote mental health and well-being.   .

Conclusion

As we've explored throughout this book, solitude is a powerful tool for personal growth, creativity, and mental well-being. By incorporating solitude into our daily lives, we can reduce stress, increase productivity, and cultivate a deeper sense of self-awareness.

Whether you're looking to improve your mental health, boost your creativity, or simply find more balance in your life, solitude can be a valuable ally. By taking the time to reflect on your thoughts, feelings, and experiences, you can gain a deeper understanding of yourself and the world around you.

As you move forward on your journey, remember that solitude is not about isolating yourself from others, but about taking care of yourself and nurturing your mind, body, and spirit. By prioritizing solitude, you can cultivate a more positive, resilient, and fulfilling life. So take the first step today, and start incorporating solitude into your daily routine. Whether it's taking a quiet walk, practicing meditation, or simply spending time in nature, make solitude a priority and watch your life transform in powerful ways.